1

~Introducing Fiqh Series~
Vol.8

Introducing the Fiqh of Food and Drink

(فقه الأطعمة و الأشربة)

Written and compiled by
SAFARUK Z. CHOWDHURY

AD-DUHA
LONDON 2009

First edition 2009

Updated Edition 2012

An educational publication from Ad-Duha London
Third Floor, 42 Fieldgate Street
London E1 1ES
E: info@duha.org.uk
W: www.duha.org.uk
T: 07891 421 925

TABLE OF ABBREVIATIONS

Art.   = article

Bk.   = book

pp.   = pages

`   = the Arabic letter ع

'   = the Arabic letter ء

هـ .إ   = 'end of quote' where a cited textual segment in Arabic ends.

s: = additional comments made by the translator

Table of Symbols

\#   = *hadith* number

(…)   = contains transliteration of Arabic terms

[…]   = contains additions by the translator

… / [...] = ellipsis where a textual segment is elided and omitted in translation by the translator

{...}   = enclosure of a Qur'anic verse in translation

§   = section

4

Contents Page

Chapter and Section:	Page
Table of Abbreviations	3
Table of Symbols	3
§1. Introduction	5-8
§2. Preliminaries: Relevant *Qawa`id* (legal maxims)	8-11
§3. Meats and Fish	11-21
§4. Fruits, Vegetables and Baking Products	21-22
§5. Dairy Products, Confectionary, Condiments, Oils and Dried Food	22-24
§6. General Beverages	24
§7. Prawns – Legal Discussion	25
§8. Crow – Legal Discussion	25-26
§9. Eels – Legal Discussion	27-29
§10. *Nabidh* (fermented beverages) and Synthetic Alcohol	29-38
§11. Miscellaneous Rulings	38-42
Key References	43-45

THE BASIC *FIQH* OF FOOD AND DRINKS

الحمد لله حمداً يبلغ رضاه وصلى الله على أشرف من اجتباه
وعلى من صاحبه ووالاه وسلم تسليماً لا يدرك منتهاه.

Praise be to Allah Most High; The
Giver of this perfect and final Law
for all times and abundant blessings
upon our beloved Prophet, the
Divine Mercy sent for humankind
who embodied this perfect Law and
implemented it for all to follow and
who is the Light of guidance that
has radiated the firmaments.
Blessings too upon his noble
companions who followed His
blessed example in implementing
this sacred law, his pure family and
all those who follow them in creed
and deed until the Final Day. To
proceed:

§1. Introduction

- Our law is sacred because it is From Allah (swt).[1]

- Our Sacred Law is the most perfect legal system
because it is from Allah (swt).[2]

---

[1] Shah `Abd al-Haqq al-Dihlawi, *Takmil al-Iman*, p.101.
[2] Shah `Abd al-Haqq al-Dihlawi, *Takmil al-Iman*, p.101.

- Our Sacred Law has abrogated all previous legal systems and indeed our *din* has abrogated all earlier religions.[3]

- It is the view of all *usuli* scholars as well as theologians that the human mind (`aql*) cannot ascertain what is right and what is wrong related to moral actions and indeed any action.[4]

- It is also the view of the *usuli* scholars that legal injunctions and rulings pertaining to food and drinks may often elude rational evaluations and so the believer takes these on the utter conviction and trust that the Lawgiver – Allah (swt) – has legislated them in the general best interest of human beings and that there is wisdom (*hikam*) underpinning them.

- The same point extends to the blessed example (*sunnah*) of humanity's greatest blessing (and indeed that of all creation) the beloved of Allah our beloved the Messenger of Allah (may the abundant peace and blessings of Allah be upon him).

- Hence, our immediate consternation of being unable to determine any sense or coherence upon coming to know the relevant legal injunctions and rulings does not warrant the inference that they neither have coherence nor are they practically enforceable. *We listen and we obey.*

- It is also our conviction that our legal tradition has been delineated by the greatest legal minds and personalities unrivalled in any civilisation.

---

[3] Shah `Abd al-Haqq al-Dihlawi, *Takmil al-Iman*, p.147.
[4] al-Nabhani, *al-Shakhsiyya al-Islmamiyya*, 3:14-18.

- We believe that our noble scholar-jurists (*mujtahidun* and *fuqaha'*) were:

    1. Trustworthy.
    2. Qualified.
    3. Pious.
    4. Sincere.
    5. But fallible.

- Moreover, we approach the study of the *fiqh* with humility and reverence but with a critical engagement of this legacy. And may Allah enable us to carry out the tasks required of us. *Amin.*

- This is a small booklet outlining some very basic legal injunctions and rulings pertaining to the consumption of food and drink as found within the School (*madhhab*) of the noble Imam Abu Hanifa Nu`man ibn Thabit (80-150/768) – may Allah be pleased with him. There is no extensive analysis nor are their comparative discussions and evaluations although some *fiqh* discussions are given of some common questions surrounding food types and their consumption. It is hoped that this small contribution helps those who read it and nothing is asked of them except sincere *du`as.*

- Much is omitted here in this booklet such as the following to mention but a few:

    1. The rulings pertaining to the slaughter of animals (*al-dhaba'ih*).

2. The rulings pertaining to labelling, packaging and delivery of food and drink products.

3. The rulings pertaining to food hygiene.

4. The rulings pertaining to the manners of eating and drinking.

5. Rulings pertaining to ethical consumerism.

6. Details of the evidential merits and derivations made by the various jurists.

- Below is the summary content topics of this small booklet.

§2. Preliminaries:
Some Relevant *Qawa`id Fiqhiyyah* (Legal Maxims)

- Some operating legal maxims (*qawa`id fiqhiyya*) related to this section of *fiqh* include amongst many others the following:

الأصل في الأشياء الإباحة حتى يدل الدليل على التحريم:

1. **The legal norm is that**: All things and objects (e.g. food, clothes, utensils, drinks, etc.) are lawful until proven to the contrary through legal evidence. Therefore the operating assumption is that all objects not yet existent unless already prohibited are permitted unless legal evidence restricts either their use, consumption, usufruct or trade.[5]

---

[5] al-Zuhayli, *al-Qawa`id al-Fiqhiyya*, 1:189-192.

9

الأصل براءة الذمة:

2. **The legal norm is that**: one is in a condition of non-liability (i.e. a presumed state of innocence and free of guilt). One is not obligated to prove anything and so the operating assumption is that one is free from assertions of guilt and wrongful charges.[6]

الأصل العدم:

3. **The legal norm is that**: one is in a state of non-existent liability. Thus, the operating assumption is that one is free from any legal liability and is not required to affirm this status – it is on-going. Thus, unless there is compelling legal reason to assume otherwise, a person's offerings of food and drink is assumed to be *halal*.[7]

كل رخصة أبيحت للضرورة والحاجة لم تستبح قبل وجودها:

4. **The legal norm is that**: legal dispensations permit what is otherwise unlawful due to necessity or strong need but this does not mean in origin it was permitted. Thus, it may not be inferred that just because the Law offers express permission to consume alcohol and pig meat due to exceptional cases, this dispensation is something permitted in origin.[8]

---

[6] al-Zuhayli, *al-Qawaʿid al-Fiqhiyya*, 1:141-145.
[7] al-Zuhayli, *al-Qawaʿid al-Fiqhiyya*, 1:188-189.
[8] al-Zuhayli, *al-Qawaʿid al-Fiqhiyya*, 1:296.

- Below are some basic food categories as discussed in the books of *Fiqh*:

General Food Categories

1. Meat (e.g. white meat and red meat, etc.)	2. Fish (includes fresh, packaged, dried and raw)	3. Fruits (natural and packaged)	4. Vegetables (natural and packaged)	5. Dairy (all produce natural or processed)
6. Bakery (e.g. bread, cakes, etc.)	7. Confectionary (e.g. sweets, savouries, etc.)	8. Condiments (e.g. sauces, spices, relishes, dry herbs and seasonings, etc.)	9. Fats and oils (e.g. butter, lard, grease, etc.)	10. Dried foods (e.g. pasta, cereals, grains, maize, wheat, oats, muesli, etc.)

General Beverage Categories

11. Juices (e.g. squeezed, artificially mixed, etc.)	12. Soft drinks (includes all fizzy drinks...)	13. Hot beverages (e.g. tea, coffee, hot chocolate, etc.)	14. Dairy drinks (e.g. UHT products, milk, yogurt, milkshakes, etc.)	15. Alcoholic (e.g. wines, spirits, beers, etc.).

- Categorising food and drink is a matter of taxonomy (classification) which is determined through an item having shared properties and realities. Therefore, it would be cumbersome and indeed impossible to list an exhaustive catalogue of permissible and impermissible foods and drinks. Hence in what follows there will only be general rulings (*ahkam shar'iyya*) related to food and drink types/categories and the legal criteria in determining their lawfulness or unlawfulness as laid down by the noble *fuqaha'* of the Hanafi School.

§3. Category 1 & 2: Meats & Fish

- In the *Mukhtasar* of Imam al-Quduri (d. 428/1037), the basic outlines of prohibited food types is given:

ولا يجوز أكل كل ذي ناب من السباع وكل ذي مخلب من الطير ولا بأس بغراب الزرع ولا

يؤكل الأبقع الذي يأكل الجيف ويكره أكل الضبع والضب والحشرات كلها ولا يجوز أكل

لحم الحمر الأهلية والبغال ويكره لحم الفرس عند أبي حنيفة ولا بأس بأكل الأرنب وإذا

ذبح ما لا يؤكل لحمه طهر لحمه وجلده إلا الآدمي والخنزير فإن الذكاة لا تعمل فيهما ولا

يؤكل من حيوان الماء إلا السمك ويكره أكل الطافي منه ولا بأس بأكل الجريث والمارماهي

ويجوز أكل الجراد ولا ذكاة له (القدوري: المختصر صـ 572–573)

"It is not permissible to eat any canine-toothed beasts of prey [*dhu nab*; s: which includes those with fangs and wild beats], nor any taloned birds [*dhu mikhlab*; s: which includes anything that is clawed and predatory]. There is no objection to eating the agrarian crow (*ghurab al-zara'*) but the piebald one [s: speckled in colour] that eats corpses [s: perhaps referring to a magpie, carrion crow, jungle crow and species of ravens, vultures and all other scavenging birds] may not be eaten. It is *makruh* [*tahriman*] to eat the hyena [s: and anything of its species], the lizard[9] and all insects [s: including all pests and rodents]. It is not permitted to eat the meat of the domesticated donkeys and mules[10] and Abu

---

[9] Lizards (*al-dabb*) are prohibited by the Hanafis based on at least two textual evidences (both *hasan* in their *isnad*): [1] From the mother of the believers `A'isha who was prohibited from eating it when she asked the Messenger of Allah and [2] Sayyiduna Ibn `Umar who stated that it was something they used to eat but stopped doing so:

"The Prophet was asked about [eating] the lizard and he forbade it..." Ibn Hajar al-`Asqalani, *Fath al-Bari*, 9:583.	عن النبي صلى الله عليه وسلم أنه نهى عن الضب...
"Ibn `Umar was asked about [eating] lizards and he said: 'since the Prophet told us, we ended eating it'..." al-Haythami, *Majma` al-Zawa'id*, 4:40.	عن ابن عمر أنه سئل عن الضب فقال أنا منذ قال فيه رسول الله صلى الله عليه وسلم ما قال فإنا قد انتهينا عن أكله...

[10] In *al-Lubab fi Sharh al-Kitab*, 3:96 of al-Ghunaymi, it has:

لأنها متولدة من الحمر فكانت مثلها . قيد بالأهلية لأن الوحشية حلال وإن صارت أهلية وإن نزا أحدهما على الآخر فالحكم للأم كما في النظم قهستاني (الغنيمي، اللباب في شرح الكتاب جـ 3 ص 396)

"[The reason why the mule is also not permitted to eat] is because it is born from a donkey and so is considered the same as it. The reason why the author restricted the reference to horses and mules to 'domesticated' (*ahliyya*) is because if they are wild (*wahshiyya*) then it is permitted to eat them even if it later becomes domesticated. If both are bred together [s: if a jack, i.e. male donkey is bred with a mare, i.e. a female horse] then it takes the ruling of its mother as mentioned *al-Nazm*; refer to al-Quhistani..."

Hanifa considers the horse meat to be *makruh*.[11] There is no harm in eating rabbits. Fish may only be eaten from the sea but it is *makruh* to eat fish that are dead and floating on the water (*al-tafi*). *Jirrith* and eels too may be eaten as well as locusts and for the latter no slaughter is necessary."[12]

- In the Hanafi compendium of legal verdicts entitled *al-Fatawa al-Hindiyya* it has the following divisions and categories of lawful food:

الْحَيَوَانُ فِي الْأَصْلِ نَوْعَانِ نَوْعٌ يَعِيشُ فِي الْبَحْرِ وَنَوْعٌ يَعِيشُ فِي الْبَرِّ أَمَّا الذي يَعِيشُ فِي

الْبَحْرِ فَجَمِيعُ ما فِي الْبَحْرِ مِن الْحَيَوَانِ يَحْرُمُ أَكْلُهُ إلَّا السَّمَكُ خَاصَّةً فإنه يَحِلُّ أَكْلُهُ إلَّا ما

طَفَا منه وَأَمَّا الذي يَعِيشُ فِي الْبَرِّ فَأَنْوَاعٌ ثَلَاثَةٌ ما ليس له دَمٌ أَصْلًا وما ليس له دَمٌ سَائِلٌ وما

له دَمٌ سَائِلٌ (الفتاوى الهندية جـ 5 ص 289)

---

[11] In *al-Lubab fi Sharh al-Kitab*, 3:96 of al-Ghunaymi, it has the comments:

قال الإمام الإسبيجابي : الصحيح أنها كراهة تنزيه وفي الهداية وشرح الزاهدي : ثم قيل : الكراهة عنده كراهة

تحريم وقيل : كراهة تنزيه والأول أصح وقالا : لا بأس بأكله ورجحوا دليل الإمام واختاره المحبوبي والنسفي

والموصلي وصدر الشريعة تصحيح (الغنيمي، اللباب في شرح الكتاب جـ 3 ص 396)

"Imam al-Isbijabi said: The correct understanding is that it is disliked at the level of *tanzih* (merely disliked) and in *al-Hidaya* and the *Sharh* of al-Zahidi it has: and the level of *karaha* according to him [s: meaning Abu Hanifa] is that of *tahrim* [s: i.e. it is prohibited to eat]. It is also said: the level of *karaha* is that of *tanzih*. The first however is more correct. They both said: there is no harm in eating it although the evidence of the Imam was preferred for example by al-Mahbubi, al-Nasafi, al-Mawsili and Sadr al-Shari`a..."

[12] See al-Quduri, *al-Mukhatasr*, pp.572-573.

"In origin, two types of creatures or animals are lawful to eat; one type that lives in sea and one type that lives on land. As for what lives in the sea, everything except fish is prohibited to eat as long as that is not floating dead on the water surface. And as for what lives on land, there are three types: [1] that which does not essentially have blood; [2] that which does not have flowing blood and [3] that which has flowing blood [...] and whatever has flowing blood is of two types: [1] domesticated or the common animal (*al-musta'nas*) and [2] wild animals (*al-mutawahhish*) and [...] the common or domesticated animal can be canine-toothed like a dog [...] and the wild animal/creature can be a canine-toothed beast as well as a taloned bird [of prey] or [...] a non-taloned bird that is domesticated like a chicken..."[13]

- Meats are therefore divided by the Law into [1] dead and [2] living:

Dead animals (unlawful for consumption):	Living animals (that are unlawful for consumption):
1. Carrion.	1. **Any and all animals/creatures explicitly forbidden by the Qur'an or the Prophet**, e.g. swine, donkey[15], mules,[16] Lizards, etc.
2. Carcasses.	
3. Non-slaughtered meat of dead animals.	

---

[13] See *al-Fatawa al-Hindiyya*, 5:289. This is based on the *hadith* in Bukhari's *Sahih* (#5780) where the Messenger of Allah (saw) said: "...prohibited is the eating of all fanged beasts of prey, and all the birds having talons."

[15] See the *hadiths* in Bukhari, *Sahih* (#5202, 5205 & 5208).

4. Sacrificed animals from other religious traditions.

Aspects of a lawful animal impermissible to eat include:

a. Its flowing blood (whether from the heart, liver, spleen, arteries/veins).

b. Its urinary tract (male and female animals).

c. Testicles.

d. Anus.

e. Glands.

f. Bladder.

g. Gall bladder.

h. Intestines.

i. Spinal marrow.[14]

2. **All animals that are born and live in water other than fish**, e.g. *aquatic* crustaceans like:

   a. Jellyfish.
   b. Crabs.
   c. Crayfish.
   d. Lobsters.
   e. Prawn.
   f. Shrimp. etc.

3. All animals/creatures that:

[a] **have no blood in them**, e.g. all insects like spiders, ants, flies, etc. The exception is locust due to the *hadith* of the Messenger of Allah;[17]

[b] **predatory insects** like scorpions;

[c] *terrestrial crustaceans* (crabs and woodlice) and

[d] **Molluscs** like:

---

[16] See Abu Dawud, *Sunan* (#3790) and Ahmad's *Musnad*, 4/89.

[14] See al-Shaybani, *Kitab al-Athar* (#811) and Mufti Ludianvi, *Ahsan al-Fatawa*, 7:406 and Mufti Lajpuri, *Fatawa Rahimiyya*, 2:183-185. All these aspects are considered *khaba'ith* (filth) as understood from the verse {*...and He allows for them what is pure and good and disallows for them what is filthy...* [Q. 5:157]}.

[17] See Abu Dawud, *Sunan* (#3806):

     a. Squids.
     b. Clams.
     c. Mussels.
     d. Oysters.
     e. Octopus.
     f. Scallops.
     g. Snails.
     h. Slugs, etc.

4. **All land creatures that do not have flowing blood**, e.g. reptiles like lizards, chameleons, snakes, turtles, etc.

5. **All creatures considered rodents** (*hasharat al-ard*), e.g. rats, mice, gerbils, squirrels, porcupines, etc.

6. **All terrestrial predatory animals** (i.e. that hunt with their teeth), e.g. wild beasts like elephants, lions, tigers, leopards, cheetahs, hyenas, foxes, dogs, cats, etc.

7. **All predatory birds** (i.e. that hunt with their claws/talons) such as hawks, falcons, eagles,

---

From Ibn Abi Awfa: "I fought with the Messenger of Allah (Allah bless him & give him peace) in six or seven battles, and we used to eat it [s: i.e. locust] with him."

vultures, kites, owls, etc.[18]

- Thus, in general for adherents of the Hanafi *madhhab*, sea-food other than fish must be eaten with caution ensuring that they are verified as non-prohibited items.

Permitted types of meat and fish

Animal Meat (lawful for consumption):	Fish meat (lawful for consumption):
1. **Animals that are non-predatory and terrestrial** (i.e. feed on leaves and grass or grazes), like the following are permitted to eat: a. Cows. b. Sheep. c. Goats. d. Camel. e. Deer. f. Buffalos. g. Bison. h. Horse.	1. **All categories/types of fish are lawful to consume** (including eels, whale and sharks) such as the following: a. Anchovy. b. Basa. c. Bass. d. Catfish. e. Carp. f. Cod. g. Grouper. h. Haddock. i. Halibut. j. Herring.

[18] Based on the *hadith* in Muslim, *Sahih* (#1934):

From Ibn `Abbas: "...the Messenger of Allah (Allah bless him & give him peace) prohibited the eating of all fanged beasts of prey and all the birds having talons."

i. Rabbits.

2. **Birds that are non-predatory and eat grains and crops** like the following below are permitted to eat:

a. Chicken.
b. Ducks.
c. Pigeons.
d. Sparrows.
e. Dove.
f. Crow.
g. Pheasants.
h. Parrots.
i. Partridge.
j. Turkey.
k. Lark.
l. Rooster.
m. Stalk.
n. Peacock.
o. Goose.
p. Heron.
q. Quails.
r. Ostrich.[19]

3. **Animals that consume impure things** to the extent that it creates bad/foul traces of odour in its meat and milk, then it will be

k. Mackerel.
l. Perch.
m. Pike.
n. Pollock.
o. Salmon.
p. Sardine.
q. Shark.
r. Snapper.
s. Sole.
t. Swordfish.
u. Tilapia.
v. Trout.
w. Tuna.

2. **Fish that has died due to an external cause** are lawful to consume such as:

a. Colliding with something.
b. Heat.
c. Cold.
d. Washed up on shore, etc.

3. **Fish that floats on water** (*samak al-tafi*) is not lawful based on the *hadiths* mentioned about it.[21]

---

[19] An ostrich is a non-predatory bird that is a plant-eater and therefore permitted to eat. See *al-Fatawa al-Hindiyya*, 5:289 for the criterion.

makruh (disliked) to consume its meat and drink its milk.[20]

Why do the Hanafi *Fuqaha'* restrict seafood to only fish?

Legal analysis:

Reason one: [1] The verse {*Lawful for you is the sayd al-bahr and its food is a benefit for you and those who travel with you and prohibited to you is the sayd al-barr if you are in a state of ihram; and so be mindful of Allah to Whom you will be raised up again*} must be taken in its literal sense.[22]

The word *sayd* can mean: [1] 'hunting' (*ism masdar*/the verbal noun) or [2] all that is caught from the water (i.e. 'what is hunted') thus taking the objective sense (*maf'ul lahu*).[23] If we take the first meaning, we have:

---

[21] See for example, *Sunan* of Abu Dawud (#3809):

From Jabir ibn 'Abd Allah: "What the sea throws up and is left by the tide you may eat, but what dies in the sea and floats you must not eat."

[20] Ibn 'Abidin, *Radd al-Muhtar*, 1:346:

وفي الملتقى المكروه الجلالة التي إذا قربت وجد منها رائحة فلا تؤكل ولا يشرب لبنها ولا يعمل عليها ويكره

بيعها وهبتها وتلك حالها (ابن عابدين، رد المحتار جـ 1 ص 346)

"And in *al-Multaqa* it has: the disliked form of *jallala* [s: a word that means an animal becoming impure due to either feeding or fed unclean things] is when it comes near, an odour is found from it. This meat cannot be eaten nor can its milk be consumed; it may not be used nor given as a present in that condition..."

[22] Because: "In the case of a word, the sense, in which it is presumed to be used, is the literal sense" (art. 12), *Mejelle-Ahkam-i 'Adliyye*.

[23] See al-Tabari, *al-Jami' al-Bayan*, 10:57-58, where it states:

{Lawful for you is <u>hunting in the sea</u> and its food is a benefit for you and those who travel with you and prohibited to you is the <u>hunting on land</u> if you are in a state of ihram; and so be mindful of Allah to Whom you will be raised up again}. If we take the second meaning we have: *{Lawful for you is <u>everything caught (hunted) from the sea</u> and its food is a benefit for you and those who travel with you and prohibited to you is <u>everything caught (hunted) on land</u> if you are in a state of ihram; and so be mindful of Allah to Whom you will be raised up again}*. But this second meaning of '*and prohibited to you is <u>everything caught (hunted) on land</u> if you are in a state of ihram*' is clearly incorrect as it is permitted by the Law for any pilgrim (*muhrim*) to eat animals whether wild or hunted as long as the person in the state of *ihram* did not hunt it himself. Thus, this is the compelling/contextual indication (*qarina*) that the meaning of the word *sayd* is 'hunting' and not 'whatever is caught from the sea'/'hunted'. And the operating *fiqh* principle is that words are taken in their ostensive literal sense and not their metaphorical sense.

Reason two: [2] The word *ta'am* (طعام) means: 'food' and can here in the verse refer to every food category in the sea. The pronoun *–hu* ('he'/'it') refers back to *bahr* (بحر/ 'ocean'/'sea' – although in fact it can mean any large water such as rivers, lakes, streams, etc. where one can sea-hunt

---

حدثنا ابن بشار، قال: ثنا عبد الرحمن بن مهدي، قال: ثنا سفيان، عن أبي حصين، عن سعيد بن جبير: { أُحِلَّ لَكُمْ صَيْدُ الْبَحْرِ } قال: السمك الطريّ.

"Ibn Bashshar told us that: `Abd al-Rahman b. Mahdi told us that: Sufyan told us from Abu Hasin from Sa`id b. Jubayr that: *{lawful for you is the <u>sayd al-bahr</u> [sea-hunting]}* refers to fresh fish of that sea (*al-samak al-tari)...*"

in).[24] However, there is a *hadith* that restricts or specifies what exactly can be eaten from the sea/ocean:

The Prophet said: "[...] **'the sea-water is pure and its carrion (*maytata*) is lawful to eat'**..."[25] However, the 'carrion/*maytata*' of the sea was then qualified by another statement: **"Two carrions and two bloods have been made lawful for us: The locust and the fish as well as the liver and the spleen..."**[26] Thus, from the *hadiths* just mentioned, fish are described as 'carrion' (*maytata*) and so in the context of the sea, refers only to fish. This also excludes them from the general prohibition in the verse {*Unlawful for you [to eat] is carrion, blood and the flesh of swine...* [Q. 5:3]}. Therefore, whatever is permitted from the sea/ocean is fish (*al-samak*). And Allah knows best.

§4. Category 3, 4 & 6: Fruits, Vegetables and Bakery Products

- All fruits, all vegetables and all bakery products are permitted (*halal*) to eat unless due to the following:

  1. They are explicitly forbidden by text (*nass*).

  2. They are not poisonous/harmful to the body.

---

[24] al-Shawkani, *Fath al-Qadir*, 1:178.
[25] Abu Dawud, *Sunan* (#83):

سأل رجل النبي صلى الله عليه وسلم فقال يا رسول الله إنا نركب البحر ونحمل معنا القليل من الماء فإن توضأنا به عطشنا أفنتوضأ بماء البحر فقال رسول الله صلى الله عليه وسلم هو الطهور ماؤه الحل ميتته

[26] See al-Bayhaqi, *Sunan al-Kubra*, 1:254 and his *Sunan al-Sughra*, 1:254:

عن عبد الله بن عمر أنه قال : أحلت لنا ميتتان ودمان : الجراد والحيتان، والكبد والطحال

3. They are no mixed with unlawful items of food or ingredients.

4. They are specific offerings for religious sacrifice or ritual.

§5. Category 5, 7-10: Dairy products, Confectionary, Condiments, Oils and Dried Foods

- Below is a table of basic or common food items of the above categories:

1] Dairy Products (dried, frozen or natural produced from cows or domesticated buffalos):

1. Milk.
2. Butter.
3. Cheese.
4. Yogurts.
5. Ice-cream

2] Confectionary (high sugar content foods with low nutritional value):

1. Chocolates.
2. Fudge.
3. Toffee.
4. Candy.
5. Hard sweets.
6. Nougat.
7. Liquorice.
8. Marzipan

3] Condiments (natural, fresh or packaged):

1. Salts.
2. Peppers.
3. Spices.
4. Sauces.
5. Olive oil.
6. Relish.
7. Mayonnaise
8. Vinegar.

4] Fats and Oils (liquid, solid, processed):

1. Ghee.
2. Butter.
3. Lard.
4. Margarine.
5. Cooking oils.

a. Almond oil.
b. Walnut oil.
c. Rapeseed.
d. Peanut oil.
e. Mustard oil.
f. Olive oil.
g. Sunflower oil.
h. Sesame oil.
i. Corn oil.
j. Coconut oil.

- With regard to dairy products, confectionary, condiments, oils and dried foods, they are all permitted to eat as long as:

1. Any animal/bird ingredients are from those slaughtered according to the method of our Sacred Law.
2. All ingredients are from animals/birds lawful to eat.
3. All products are not mixed with unlawful items of food and drink.

- The same ruling also holds for food additives, preservatives, flavours, enhancers, colourings, etc. (including all chemical and industry E numbers) such as:

1. Rennet (although there is difference about this in the Hanafi School).
2. Glycerine.
3. Gelatine.
4. Lactose.
5. Whey.

§6. Category 11-15: General Beverages

- All beverages (*ashriba*) are permitted for consumption as long as the following general conditions are met:

1. They contain **no** alcohol (*khamr*).

2. They are not mixed with unlawful and harmful chemicals (e.g. drugs).

3. They are not produced with unlawful ingredients.

§7. Prawns – what's in a Fish?

- The Hanafi *fuqaha'* have differed over the permissibility of eating prawns and shrimps. The point being due to the disagreement over whether it is classified as either a fish (*samak*) or a non-fish according to the Arabs at the time of revelation.

- For those who hold it to be classed as a fish, then its consumption is no doubt permissible. This appears to be the stronger opinion of the Hanafi School as also evaluated by contemporary scholars.[27]

- For those who do not consider it not to be a fish give the ruling that it is a crustacean and therefore like lobsters impermissible to eat (*makruh tahrimi*).[28]

- Thus, it is a difference of taxonomy. And Allah knows best.

---

[27] See for example:

1. "Are Prawns Halal According to the Hanafi's?" at http://qa.sunnipath.com/issue_view.asp?HD=7&ID=443&CATE=29;
2. "Vinegar and Prawns" at http://www.albalagh.net/qa/vinegar_prawns.shtml and
3. "What is Halal" at http://askimam.org/fatwa/fatwa.php?askid=d04013b28a21924be02997357a7cff54

[28] Alahazrat Imam Ahmad Reza Khan, *al-Fatawa al-Ridwiyya*, and idem, *Ahkam-e-Shariat*, part 1 available at http://www.razanw.org/modules/products/item.php?itemid=36 and Mufti Taqi Usmani, *Dars-e-Tirmizi*, pp.278-84.

§8. Crows? – Depends on Types

- There are qualifications regarding eating crows in the Hanafi School as mentioned by Imam Ibn al-Nujaym in *al-Bahr al-Ra'iq*:

قال رحمه الله : (وحل غراب الزرع) لأنه يأكل الحب وليس من سباع الطير ولا من

الخبائث قال رحمه الله : (لا الأبقع – الذي يأكل الجيف – والضبع والضب والزنبور

والسلحفاة والحشرات والحمر الأهلية والبغل) يعني : هذه الأشياء لا تؤكل أما الغراب

الأبقع فلأنه يأكل الجيف فصار كسباع الطير والغراب ثلاثة أنواع : نوع يأكل الجيف

فحسب فإنه لا يؤكل، ونوع يأكل الحب فحسب فإنه يؤكل، ونوع يخلط بينهما وهو أيضا

يؤكل عند الإمام وهو العقعق لأنه يأكل الدجاج وعن أبي يوسف أنه يكره أكله لأنه غالب

أكله الجيف، والأول أصح (إبن النجيم، البحر الرائق ج8 ص 172)

"He, Allah have mercy on him, said: (**The field crow is permitted to eat**) because it eats grains and is not classified as a predatory bird nor is it classified as a filthy creature. He Allah have mercy on him said: (**but the piebald [s: i.e. patterned in its colour] bird is not permitted to eat**) which eats carrion [s: like the piebald eagle or certain vultures] nor is the lizard, hyena, wasps, tortoise, insects, donkeys and mules, i.e. they are not eaten. As for the crow that eats carrion, it is considered a predatory bird and so may not be eaten. Thus, the crow is of three types: [1] one type that eats carrion so consuming it is unlawful; [2] the other type is one that eats grains and so this is permitted to consume and [3] one type that is a mix of both which is like the magpie (*al-`aq`aq*) that eats little chicken and that too is permissible to eat according the Imam but according to Abu Yusuf it is disliked because it eats more carrion than non-carrion but the first opinion is more correct."[29]

§9. Eels – 'No eel Problems Here'

- In the book *Hayat al-Hayawan* by al-Damiri, 1:225 it has under 'eel' the following:

الجريث: بكسر الجيم بالراء المهملة والثاء المثلثة، وهو هذا السمك الذي يشبه الثعبان.

وجمعه جراثي. ويقال له أيضا الجريء بالكسر والتشديد وهو نوع من السمك يشبه الحية

ويسمى بالفارسية مارماهي وقد تقدم في باب الهمزة أنه الأنكليس. قال الجاحظ: إنه يأكل

الجرذان وهو حية الماء. وحكمه: الحل قال البغوي عند قوله تعالى: " أحل لكم صيد البحر

وطعامه " إن الجريث حلال بالاتفاق، وهو قول أبي بكر وعمر وابن عباس وزيد بن ثابت

وأبى هريرة رضي الله تعالى عنهم وبه قال شريح والحسن وعطاء، وهو مذهب مالك وظاهر

مذهب الشافعي. والمراد هذه الثعابين التي لا تعيش إلا في الماء. وأما الحيات التي تعيش

في البر والبحر، فتلك من ذوات السموم، وأكلها حرام. وسئل ابن عباس عن الجري فقال:

هو شيء حرمته اليهود ونحن لا نحرمه (الدامري، حياة الحيوان جـ 1 ص 225).

"'*al-Jirrith*' [...] it is a type of fish that that resembles a snake. It is also called '*al-jirri*' which is a type of fish that looks like a snake and is called in Persian '*marmahi*' [...] and its ruling is that it is permitted to eat. al-Baghawi stated from the words of Allah Most High {*permitted for you is the harvest of the sea and its food* [5:96]} that *al-jirrith* are

---

[29] Ibn al-Nujaym in *al-Bahr al-Ra'iq*, 8:172 and Alahazrat Imam Ahmad Reza Khan, *al-Fatawa al-Ridwiyya*, 20:319-320.

permitted by agreement of all the scholars and this is the opinion of Abu Bakr, `Umar, Ibn `Abbas, Zayd ibn Thabit, Abu Hurayra (May Allah be pleased with them all). Shurayh, al-Hasan, `Ata`, the position of Malik and the most apparent view of al-Shafi`i also accords with this. What these *tabi`un* intend is that which lives in the water. As for the snakes that live both in water and land, they are poisonous and to eat them is unlawful. Ibn `Abbas was asked about the *Jirri* and he replied that the Jews prohibited its consumption but we do not..."

- Imam al-Mawsili in *Kitab al-Ikhtiyar* writes:

(ولا يؤكل من حيوان الماء إلا السمك) لأنه ميتة فيحرم بالنص، وإنما حل السمك بما

روينا من الحديث وأنه يشمل جميع أنواعه الجريث والمارماهي وغيرهما (الموصلي، الإختيار

جـ 5 ص 464).

"(Creatures other than fish that live in the sea may not be eaten) because they are considered *maytata* (dead meat) which is unlawful based on text. Fish is made lawful based on what has been narrated in the *hadith* which includes all types of fish like the *jirith* (hagfish) and the *marmahi* [s: which is a type of eel fish] and others like it..."[30]

- The reason why the permissibility of eels is specifically mentioned in the *fiqh* books is for a corrective purpose as explained by al-Ghunaymi in *al-Lubab*:

---

[30] al-Mawsili in *Kitab al-Ikhtiyar*, 5:464.

قال في الدرر: و خصهما بالذكر إشارة الى ضعف ما نقل في المغرب عن محمد أن جميع
السمك حلال غير الجريث والمارماهي (الغنيمي، اللباب في شرح الكتاب جـ 3 ص 397)

"And the author specifically mentioned both [s: i.e. the hagfish and the eel] in order to allude to the weakness in what was transmitted about Muhammad by those in the west [s: the western Muslim lands] that he permitted all fish except *al-jirrith* and *al-marmahi*..."[31]

§10. Alcohol and Synthetic (chemical) Alcohol: 'To *Nabidh* or not to *Nabidh*!' – Some important Explanations

- According to *fuqaha'* of the Hanafi School, alcohol is of two general types:

[1] Alcohol derived from...

1. Dates (*tamr*).

2. Grapes (`*inab*).

= *khamr* and is categorically *haram* whether one takes a little (1 drop) or a lot (1 glass) or whether it actually intoxicates or not.

This may not be used for cooking, consumption, trade or storage.

[2] Alcohol derived from...

1. Wheat.
2. Maize.
3. Oats.
4. Barley.
5. Honey.
6. Rice.
7. Malts.
8. Apple.
9. Peach.
10. Sugar cane.

= non-*khamr* or *nabidh*[32] drinks that are lawful for consumption as long as:

---

[31] al-Ghunaymi, *al-Lubab*, 3:97.

[32] See for example: D. M. Hawke (trans.), *The Life and Works of Jahiz*, §8-9, pp.52-55; P Heine, "Nabidh", *EI*, 7:840 and A. J. Wensinck and J.

1. One is not inebriated.

2. The amount of the alcohol is such that it cannot inebriate.

3. The amount that can inebriate is not mixed with anything else.

4. One does not drink out of vain/folly (*lahw*).

5. One does not intend to resemble the open sinners (*fussaq*).

All these may be used for cooking, trade, storage or other permissible uses.

- Mufti Taqi Usmani states the following in his completing commentary on Mufti Shabbir Ahmad Usmani's *Fath al-Mulhim*:[33]

القسم الثالث: الأشربة المسكرة الأخرى، غير الأقسام الأربعة المذكورة، مثل التمر أو الزبيب المطبوخ أدنى طبخة، أو عصير العنب المطبوخ الذى ذهب ثلثاه، وكذلك نبيذ العسل، والحنطة، والشعير، الحبوب الأخرى . وحكم هذا القسم عند أبى حنيفة وأبى

Sadan, "Khamr", *EI*, 4:994-997 (part printed in "Wine in Islam", *Muslim World* 18 (1928), pp.365-373.

[33] Mufti Taqi Usmani, *Takmila Fath al-Mulhim*, 3:338. See also Ibn `Abidin, *Radd al-Muhtar*, 6:452 and *al-Fatawa al-Hindiyya*, 5:414.

يوسف، رحمهما الله، أنه لا يحرم منه شرب القليل الذى لا يسكر، وإنما يحرم منه القدر

المسكر ... وبهذا يتبين حكم الكحول المسكرة التى عمت بها البلوى اليوم، فإنها تستعمل

فى كثير من الأدوية والعطور ، والمركبات الأجرى، فإنها إن اتخذت من العنب أو التمر فلا

سبيل إلى حلتها أو طهارتها، وإن اتخذت من غيرهما فالأمر فيها سهل على مذهب أبى

حنيفة رحمه الله تعالى ، ولا يحرم استعمالها للتداوى أو لأغراض مباحة أخرى ما لم تبلغ حد

الإسكار، لأنها إنما تستعمل مركبة مع المواد الأخرى، ولا يحكم بنجاستها أخذا بقول أبى

حنيفة رحمه الله . وأن معظم الكحول التى تستعمل اليوم فى الأدوية والعطور وغيرها لا تتخذ

من العنب أو التمر، إنما تتخذ من الحبوب أو القشور أو البترول وغيره، كما ذكرنا فى باب

بيع الخمر من كتاب البيوع، وحينئذ هناك فسحة فى الأخذ بقول أبى حنيفة عند عموم

البلوى، والله سبحانة أعلم (تقي عثماني، تكملة فتح الملهم جـ 5 ص 414)

"The third category: other types of intoxicating drinks that are not of the other four types mentioned such as dates or cooked raisins in a small earthen pot or cooked grape juice where three of its characteristics have gone or drink made from honey or wheat, barley and other grains. The ruling of Abu Hanifa and Abu Yusuf – may Allah have mercy on them – is that this category of drink is permitted as long as one drinks to the extent that he is not inebriated. [...] From this it becomes clear that the ruling regarding intoxicating alcohol types that are commonly and widely used today in medicines, fragrances as well as other ingredients is that if it is derived from grapes or dates then it is explicitly unlawful and impure but if it is derived from other than these two then the matter can be easily resolved according to the School of Abu Hanifa may Allah have mercy on him. It would be permitted to use these alcohols for medicinal purposes as well as any other permitted aim as long as it is not a quantity that inebriates because they are used with other substances and materials that cannot be ruled as impure based on the opinion of Abu Hanifa – Allah have mercy on him. Indeed, much of the alcohol used today in medicines, perfumes and fragrances as well as other products are not derived from dates and grapes but are derived from grain, cobalt and oils and other such substances which we have mentioned in the Chapter on trading with *khamr* in the Book of 'Buying and Selling' where there is a avenue for adopting the opinion of Abu Hanifa due to widespread need of the people (`umum al-balwa*)...*"[34]

- It is this second category of alcohol as outlined above in the table and the Arabic excerpt that has been a point of legal controversy and heated difference between scholars of the Hanafi *maslak* and those following al-Shafi`i, Malik and Ahmad (Allah be pleased with them all). This discussion has arisen again due to the re-adoption of Abu Hanifa's opinion on this matter as it conveniently allows for addressing a need within manufacture and produce. However, I believe this discussion is best left within the great legal works and not openly and adventurously discussed without proper intention (*niyya*), sincerity (*ikhlas*), fear (*khawf*), *taqwa* and correct training in the evidences. And to Allah we turn for help.

---

[34] The term `umum al-balwa* refers to a category of widespread hardship (*haraj*) people face that cannot be avoided. See Ibn al-Nujaym, *al-Ashbah al-Naza'ir*, p.85 and al-Suyuti, *al-Asbah wa'l-Naza'ir*, p.86.

Legal analysis:

- Some legal discussions have been given regarding *nabidh* by early Hanafi *fuqaha'* as for example famously by Imam al-Tahawi (d. 321/933) in his *Sharh Ma`ani al-Athar*:

ثنا أحمد بن يونس قال : ثنا ابن شهاب، عن أبي ليلى، عن عيسى، أن أباه بعثه إلى أنس

في حاجة، فأبصر عنده طلاء شديدا، والطلاء : ما يسكر كثيره، فلم يكن ذلك عند أنس

خمرا، وإن كثيره يسكر . وثبت بما وصفنا أن الخمر عند أنس، لم يكن من كل شراب

ولكنها من خاص من الأشربة (الطحاوي، شرح معاني الآثار جـ 4 ص 213-214)

"Ahmad b. Yunis related to us that: Ibn Shihab related to us from Abu Layla from `Isa whose father went to Anas b. Malik's house for something. He saw that Anas had a strong liquor (*talla' shadid*) ... and this 'strong liquor' is something which would intoxicate if drunk in a large quantity (*kathir*) so what Anas' had was not considered *khamr* (intoxicating wine/substance) even though drinking a lot of it would intoxicate and inebriate. What is established from what we have described is that Anas had *khamr* which was not of every drink [s: that intoxicates] but it was a specific sort of beverage..."[35]

عن عبد الله بن شداد بن الهاد، عن عبد الله بن عباس قال : حرمت الخمر بعينها، والسكر

من كل شراب . فأخبر ابن عباس أن الحرمة وقعت على الخمر بعينها، وعلى السكر من

سائر الأشربة سواها . فثبت بذلك أن ما سوى الخمر التي حرمت مما يسكر كثيره، قد أبيح

---

[35] al-Tahawi, *Sharh Ma`ani al-Athar*, 4:213-214.

34

شرب قليله الذي لا يسكر (الطحاوي، شرح معاني الآثار جـ 4 ص 214)

"From `Abd Allah ibn Shaddad b. al-Had from `Abd Allah ibn `Abbas who said: '*khamr* has been prohibited for itself (*bi-`ayniha*) and intoxication from every [other] type of drink'. Ibn `Abbas informed that the prohibition of *khamr* has occurred for itself whereas for all other drinks prohibition occurs upon intoxication. What is established from this is that other than *khamr* which is prohibited, if something intoxicates if one drinks it in large quantities then it would not be permitted but a little quantity that does not intoxicate would be permitted."[36]

ونحن نشهد على الله عز وجل، أنه حرم عصير العنب إذا حدثت فيه صفات الخمر، ولا

نشهد عليه أنه حرم ما سوى ذلك إذا حدث فيه مثل هذه الصفة . فالذي نشهد على الله

بتحريمه إياه هو الخمر الذي آمنا بتأويلها، من حيث قد آمنا بتنزيلها . والذي لا نشهد على

الله أنه حرم هو الشراب الذي ليس بخمر . فما كان من خمر، فقليله وكثيره حرام، وما كان

مما سوى ذلك من الأشربة ، فالسكر منه حرام ، وما سوى ذلك منه مباح هذا هو النظر

عندنا، وهو قول أبي حنيفة، وأبي يوسف، ومحمد رحمهم الله، غير نقيع الزبيب والتمر

خاصة، فإنهم كرهوا (الطحاوي، شرح معاني الآثار جـ 4 ص 215)

"And we bear witness in Allah – Mighty and Majestic is He! – that He has prohibited the juice of grapes when the qualities of wine occur in it. We do not bear witness that He has prohibited [s: the juice from] other than that if it takes on the same qualities. Thus, that which we testify to be prohibited is the *khamr* that we all believe is understood from the verse as well as it being revealed. But what we do not bear witness in Allah that any drink that is not *khamr* was

---

[36] al-Tahawi, *Sharh Ma`ani al-Athar*, 4:214.

prohibited by Him. Whatever is from *khamr*, a lot or a little of it is prohibited whereas any other drink or beverage other than that, then it is prohibited only if it intoxicates and other than that [s: i.e. the non-*khamr* drink) is permitted. This is our stance and this is the stance of Abu Hanifa, Abu Yusuf and Muhammad [ibn al-Hasan al-Shaybani] may Allah have mercy on them all. And they specifically disliked juice form raisin and dates...”[37]

- Ibn Rushd al-Qurtubi (d. 595/1198) and Hafiz Ibn `Abd al-Barr (d. 463/1071) both helpfully summarise the matter as follows:

وقال العراقيون، ابراهيم النخعي من التابعين، وسفيان الثوري، وابن أبي ليلى، وشريك، وابن

شبرمة، وأبوحنيفة، وسائر فقهاء الكوفيين، وأكثر علماء البصريين أن المحرم من سائر الأنبذة

المسكرة هو السكر نفسه لا العين (إبن رشد، بداية المجتهد جـ 1 ص **470**)

“The `Iraqi scholars, Ibrahim al-Nakha`i from the *tabi`un*, Sufyan al-Thawri, Ibn Abi Layla, Shurayk, Ibn Shabrama, Abu Hanifa and the rest of the Kufan jurists as well as the majority of the Basran scholars agree that all *nabidh* beverages are prohibited only when they intoxicate but are not prohibited in and of themselves...”[38]

واختلف الفقهاء في سائر الأنبذة المسكرة، فقال العراقيون : إنما الحرام منها المسكر، وهو

فعل الشارب، وأما النبيذ في نفسه، فليس بحرام، ولانجس، لأن الخمر العنب (إبن عبد

البر، التمهيد في شرح الموطأ جـ 1 ص **245**)

“The jurists have differed over all the remaining types of

---

[37] al-Tahawi, *Sharh Ma`ani al-Athar*, 4:215.
[38] Ibn Rushd, *Bidayat al-Mujtahid*, 1:470.

intoxicating beverages (*al-anbidhat al-muskira*). The Iraqi scholars hold to the view that intoxicants (*muskir*) are unlawful which is the act of the drinker. But as for *nabidh* itself, it is not unlawful and neither is it impure (*najis*) because *khamr* is considered to be from grapes...”[39]

- Thus, it is not surprising that we see even early giants in the field of law and *hadith* criticism drinking *nabidh* (non-*khamr* but potentially intoxicating beverages) such as for example Waki` Ibn al-Jarrah (d. 192/812-3)[40] a pious elite in the field of *hadith* evaluation and *fiqh* making such comments as follows:

قلت لوكيع : رأيت ابن عليه يشرب النبيذ حتى يُحمل على الحمار يحتاج من يرده إلى

منزله، فقال وكيع : إذا رأيت البصري يشرب فاتهمه، وإذا رأيت الكوفي يشرب فلا تتهمه .

قلت : وكيف : قال : الكوفي يشرب تدينا، والبصري يتركه تدينا (البغدادي، تاريخ بغداد ج

6 ص 237)

“I said to Waki`: I saw Ibn `Aliyya drink *nabidh* until he had to take a donkey home. Waki` said to him: ‘When you see the Basrans suspect him for it but when you see a Kufan drink it, do not suspect him for it.’ I asked: how is that? He replied: ‘the Kufan drinks it as an act of faith whereas the Basran abstains from it as an act of faith.’”[41]

---

[39] Ibn `Abd al-Barr, *al-Tamhid fi Sharh al-Muwatta'*, 1:245.
[40] al-Khattabi, *Tarikh Baghdad*, 13:472.
[41] al-Khattabi, *Tarikh Baghdad*, 6:237 (#3277) and Ibn Hajar al-`Asqalani, *Tahdhib al-Tahdhib*, 1:278.

- The point being here that each *mujtahid* is acting on what he takes to be the ruling (*hukm*) of Allah on the issue.

Related products with alcohol contents:

- White wine vinegar.
- Red wine vinegar.
- Cider vinegar.
- Balsamic vinegar.

= if made from wine then all are permitted for use as mentioned in the books of *fiqh*:

(وإذا تخللت الخمر حلت سواء صارت خلا بنفسها أو بشيء يطرح فيها، ولا يكره تخليلها) وقال الشافعي : يكره التخليل ولا يحل الخل الحاصل به إن كان التخليل بإلقاء شيء فيه قولا واحدا، وإن كان بغير إلقاء شيء فيه فله في الخل الحاصل به قولان له أن في التخليل اقترابا من الخمر على وجه التمول، والأمر بالاجتناب ينافيه ولنا قوله صلى الله عليه وسلم { نعم الإدام الخل } من غير فصل، وقوله عليه الصلاة والسلام { خير خلكم خل خمركم } ولأن بالتخليل يزول الوصف المفسد وتثبت صفة الصلاح من حيث تسكين الصفراء وكسر الشهوة، والتغذي به والإصلاح مباح، وكذا الصالح للمصالح اعتبارا بالمتخلل بنفسه وبالدباغ والاقتراب لإعدام الفساد فأشبه الإراقة، والتخليل أولى لما فيه من إحراز مال يصير حلالا في الثاني فيختاره من ابتلي به (إبن الهمام، فتح القدير جـ 9 ص 39)

"(If wine is turned into vinegar, it is permitted regardless of whether it was by itself or through something put into it

[...])"42

(وخل الخمر سواء خللت أو تخللت) يعني خل الخمر فلا فرق في ذلك بين أن يتخلل

بنفسه أو تخلل بإلقاء شيء فيه كالملح أو الخل أو النقل من الظل إلى الشمس أو بإيقاد

النار بالقرب منها خلافا للشافعي إذا تخللت بإلقاء شيء فيها كالملح ولنا قوله : عليه

الصلاة والسلام { نعم الإدام الخل } مطلقا فيتناول جميع صورها ولأن بالتخليل إزالة

الوصف المفسد وثبات صفة الصلاح كالذبائح فالتخليل أولى لما فيه من إحراز مال يصير

حلال (إبن النجيم، البحر الرائق جـ 8 ص 219)

"**(And wine vinegar [s: is permitted] whether it be from by itself or if it is mixed with something else).** i.e. wine vinegar [...] and we rely on the words of the Messenger of Allah: 'the best of condiments is vinegar' and it is absolute (*mutlaqan*) in its import and so includes all forms of it..."43

§11. General and Miscellaneous Rulings

- **Crisps with animal flavours**: If the flavouring is chemical without animal extracts unlawfully slaughtered then generally it is permitted to eat it – even if it has 'bacon flavour' on the product. However, due to possible aspersions of character doubt by Muslim onlookers, it is better to avoid.

- **Soup with prawns and shrimps**: Although there is *ikhtilaf* in the Hanafi school over prawns and shrimps, there is scope for permitting soups that

---

42 Ibn al-Hummam, *Fath al-Qadir*, 9:39.
43 Ibn al-Nujaym, *Bahr al-Ra'iq*, 8:219.

contain a small % prawns although it may be better to avoid due to the disagreement.

- **Feathers**: There is no known prohibition on consuming feathers or using them as long as it is not proven to be harmful to the consumer and so any products made from them would be permitted.[44]

- **Soya sauce**: If the ingredients are extracted from non-*khamr* sources, then it would be permitted as long as the amount does not intoxicate.

- **Apple Cider Vinegar**: it would be permitted as long as the amount does not intoxicate.

- **Medicine and alcohol**: if the medicine contains non-*khamr* alcohol (i.e. synthetic alcohol), then unless no other treatment is available, it would be permitted.[45]

- **GM foods**: It is permitted to eat genetically modified food.

- **Paan**: It is permissible to eat paan (beetle nuts with leaves).

- **Barley**: Any drink derived from barely will be permitted.

- **Chicken feet**: It is permissible to eat chicken feet.

- **Spinal cord in the neck of chicken**: it is disliked to eat it but if cooked with the meat, the meat would be *halal* to consume.

---

[44] Abu Bakr al-Jassas, *Ahkam al-Qur'an*, 1:149.
[45] Ibn `Abidin, *Radd al-Muhtar*, 1:154.

- **Yeast**: It is permitted to use and consume yeast.

- **Eating Sushi**: It is permissible to eat sushi as it is a fermented rice dish with raw fish and flavours.

- **Fish oil**: It is permissible to eat or take fish oil.

- **Gelatine**: If it is derived from a *halal* source (i.e. meat slaughtered according to Shari`a stipulations) then it would be permitted to consume. Otherwise not. If the gelatine has undergone a total chemical transformation such that its original properties are no longer present, then it would be permitted to use. However, the current cautionary *fatwa* appears to be to avoid gelatine if there is doubt regarding it.

- **Medicine and *haram* ingredients**: The general ruling is that impermissible ingredients cannot be used – even for medical purposes. However, there is a legal exemption (*rukhsa*) which is based on [1] necessity (*darura*); [2] the reasonable surety that the medicine will cure and [3] there is no known (permissible) alternative available.[46]

---

[46] Ibn `Abidin, *Radd al-Muhtar*, 1:210:

"His saying regarding (...**and the scholars have differed over using unlawful ingredients in medicine**). In the end, it is permitted if it is known to actually heal [s: and make a person better] and no other [s: lawful and] known medicines are available..."

قوله (اختلف في التداوي بالمحرم) ففي النهاية عن الذخيرة يجوز إن علم فيه شفاء ولم يعلم دواء آخر

- ***Kalima* and non-*dhabiha* food**: saying 'bismillah' before eating a non-*dhabiha* food does not make the food permissible to eat.

- **Coca-Cola**: It is permissible to drink Coca-Cola as its ethanol composition is derived or fermented from sugar cane molasses and does not intoxicate.

- **Alcohol and burn-off**: Even if alcohol is burned off during cooking, it is still not permitted to consume it.

- **Elephant meat**: It is not permissible to consume elephant meat because according to the jurists, it is classified as a predatory-like animal.[47]

- **Festive foods**: It is absolutely prohibited (and can cause one's *iman* to be compromised) if one partakes – knowingly and deliberately – in non-Muslim celebrations and festivities (e.g. Christmas, Easter, Diwali, etc.). If however, one accepts food as gifts from non-Muslims not because of the festival itself then it would be permitted but on caution better avoided (e.g. as it could have non-*halal* ingredients in them).[48]

---

[47] See Ibn Nujaym, *Bahr al-Ra'iq*, 3:63 and Ibn al-Humam, *Sharh Fath al-Qadir*, 10:510:

"And a predator is termed as any animal that normally preys, wounds, kills and transgresses..." وَالسَّبُعُ اسْمٌ لِكُلِّ مُخْتَطِفٍ مُنْتَهِبٍ جَارِحٍ قَاتِلٍ عَادٍ عَادَةً

"And the elephant is a fanged animal (*dhu nab*) and so it is *makruh* [s: *tahriman*]..." وَالْفِيلُ ذُو نَابٍ فَيُكْرَهُ

[48] See 'Alim b. 'Ala' al-Din, *al-Fatawa al-Tatarkhaniyya*, 5:355:

42

- **Textured meat**: It is permitted to eat textured meat (100% soya protein) even if it is labelled as 'pork', 'bacon', 'frankfurters' etc.

[End]

Peace and blessings upon our Master Muhammad,
His pure family, companions,
And all those who follow them
Until the Day of Judgment.

S. Z. Chowdhury
London, 2009.

"And in *al-Tatarkhaniyya*: As for what the Majus bring on their Nayruz day such as food to the elders and seniors and there is a familiarity through coming and going between them then it is said: whoever takes the food on the basis of partaking and sharing in their joy [s: and celebration], he is harming his *din*. If he accepts it not based on this, then there is no harm in taking the food although avoiding it is the more cautionary option..."

في التاترخانية: وما يأتي به المجوس في نيروزهم من الأطعمة إلى الأكابر والسادات من كانت بينهم وبينهم معرفة ذهاب ومجيء فقد قيل: إن من أخذ ذلك على وجه الموافقة لفرحهم يضر بدينه، وإن أخذه لا على ذلك الوجه لا بأس به، والاحتراز عنه أولى

KEY REFERENCES

Arabic References:

Ibn `Abidin, *Hashiyat Radd al-Muhtar `ala 'l-Durr al-Mukhtar Sharh Tanwir al-Absar*, 7 vols. Beirut: Dar al-Ihya' al-Turath al-`Arabi, n.d.

———— *Radd al-Muhtar `ala 'l-Durr al-Mukhtar*, 8 vols. Karachi: H. M. S. Co., 1986.

al-Bahlawi, *Adillat al-Hanafiyya min al-Ahadith al-Nabawiyya `ala 'l-Masa'il al-Fiqhiyya*, Damascus: Dar al-Qalam, 2007.

al-Maydani, *al-Lubab fi Sharh al-Kitab*, 4 vols. Karachi: Kutub Khana, n.d.

al-Haythami, *Majma` al-Zawa'id*, Cairo: Maktbat al-Qudsi, n.d.
———— al-Haythami, *Majma` al-Zawa'id*, Beirut: Dar al-Kitab al-`Arabi, 1982.

Ibn al-Humam, *Fath al-Qadir li 'l-`Ajiz al-Faqir Sharh al-Hidaya*, 9 vols. Beirut: Dar al-Ihya' al-Turath al-`Arabi, 1997.

al-Kasani, *al-Bada'i` al-Sana'i` fi Tartib al-Shara'i`*, 6 vols. Beirut: Dar al-Ihya' al-Turath al-`Arabi, 2000.

al-Marghinani, *al-Hidaya Sharh Bidyat al-Mubtadi*, 4 vols. Beirut: Dar al-Kutub al-`Ilmiyya, 2000.

Mawlana Nizam, et al. *al-Fatawa al-Hindiyya*, 6 vols. Quetta: Maktaba Majdiyya, 1983.

————— *al-Fatawa al-Hindiyya*, repr. Beirut: Dar al-Fikr, 1979.

————— *al-Fatawa al-Hindiyya*, 6 vols. Beirut: Dar Ihya' Turath al-`Arabi, 1980.

al-Mawsili, *Kitab al-Ikhtiyar li-Ta`lil al-Mukhtar*, 5 vols. Cairo: Dar al-Ma`rifa, 2000.

al-Nabhani, Taqi al-Din, *al-Shakhsiyya al-Islamiyya*, 3 vols. Beirut: Dar al-Umma, 2003-2005.

————— *Nizam al-Iqtisadi fi'l-Islam*, Beirut: Dar al-Umm, 2004.

al-Nadwi, S. al-*Fiqh al-Muyassar*, Karachi: Zam-Zam Publications, 2009.

Ibn Nujaym, *al-Bahr al-Ra'iq fi Sharh Kanz al-Daqa'iq*, 9 vols. Beirut: Dar al-Kutub al-`Ilmiyya, 1997.

Qadri Pasa, *al-Ahkam al-Shari'iyyah fi 'l-Ahwal al-Shakhsiyyah*, Cairo, 1924.

al-Qal`aji, M. et al, *Mu`jam al-Lughat al-Fuqaha'*, Beirut: Dar al-Nafa'is, 2000.

al-Quduri, *al-Mukhtasar* (English-Arabic text, trans. M. Kiani, London: Dar al-Taqwa, 2009).

al-Shurunbulali, *Nur al-Idah* (English-Arabic text, trans. W. Charkawi) n.p. 2004.

————— *Maraqi al-Falah Sharh Nur al-Idah*, Damascus: Maktabat al-`Ilm al-Hadith, 2001.

——— *Maraqi al-Falah Sharh Nur al-Idah*, Beirut: Dar al-Kutub al-ʿIlmiyya, 1995.

——— *Imdad al-Fattah Sharh Nur al-Idah*, Damascus, n.p. 2001.

——— *Maraqi al-Saʿadat*, Beirut: Dar al-Kutub al-Lubnani, 1973 and English trans. by F. A. Khan, London: Whitethread Press, 2010.

——— *Sabil al-Falah fi Sharh Nur al-Idah*, Beirut: Dar al-Bayruti, n.d.

Usmani, M. T. *Takmilat Fath al-Mulhim*, 3 vols. Karachi: Maktabat-i Dar al-ʿUlum, 1986-1987.

Urdu References:

Khan, Ahmed Reza. *al-ʿAtaya li-Nabawiyya fi' l-Fatawa al-Ridwiyya*, 6 vols. Mubarakpur: Sunni Darul Isha'at, 1981.

——— *al-ʿAtaya al-Nabawiyya fi' l-Fatawa al-Ridwiyya*, 12 vols. Faisalabad: Maktaba Nuriyya Ridwiyya.

Ludhianvi, Rashid Ahmad. *Ahsan al-Fatawa*, Karachi: H. M. S. Co, 1398–.

Usmani, ʿAziz al-Rahman. *ʿAziz al-Fatawa*, Karachi: Darul Isha'at, n.d.

——— *ʿAziz al-Fatawa*, 2 vols. Deoband Fatwa Department, n.d.

Printed in Great Britain
by Amazon.co.uk, Ltd.,
Marston Gate.